I0213671

More Than Just Kisses

PRESENTED BY KELLY Y. RAGIN

3G Publishing, Inc.
4495 Atlanta Highway
Loganville, Georgia 30052
www.3gpublishinginc.com
Phone: 1-888-442-9637

First published by 3G Publishing, Inc. February, 2021

ISBN: 9781941247853

Printed in the United States of America

TABLE OF CONTENTS

Dedication
Acknowledgements
Black Love
The Reynolds
The James'
The Holmes
The Taylors
The Forresters
The Johnsons
The Johnsons II
The Millers
The Hoods

Congratulations!
To The Future Mr. & Mrs. Jones

OUR LOVE
Kelly & Perry's Story

FOREWORD

By Dr. Denise Dyer

Love is still the Greatest Force in the Universe. God is Love. When you find yourself in the position to share that Powerful Force with someone else, it is truly a Blessing. I am honored to contribute to this beautiful ensemble as the writer of the foreword. As a woman who once thought of herself as super independent, my world was transformed when I met my husband at my front door. It was Saturday, February 15th, 1997. Yes, it was the day after Valentine's Day. I remember it like it was yesterday. Our union was magical from the very beginning and remained that way until he made his transition 15 years later. I'm not saying our marriage was perfect. I'm saying it was absolutely divine in its own special way. We "Loved with a Love Greater than Love." I will forever be grateful for the adventure we shared and all that I discovered in the process. When our hearts and minds are open to new experiences in our lives, God can Bless us in so many ways. Love is a Blessing. That Blessing is magnified when shared between two people who allow each other the space to honor themselves individually and collectively as a partnership. Most people don't realize that relationships allow us to heal in so many ways, on so many levels. In most cases our relationships will bring up our "stuff" of unresolved issues so we can heal and release them. Sometimes this can be a bit challenging. What's really important are the lessons learned and how we apply that new knowledge moving forward in our everyday lives and in our partnerships. At the end of the day, it's really about Love. It's about Loving ourselves enough to bring our best into our relationships for the benefit of the greater good. The couples you will meet in this book will inspire, uplift and reframe your perspective of Love. They will give you a fresh look at Black Love as they share their stories, challenges and victories.

FOREWORD CONT.

Thank you, Kelly Ragin, for the way you show up in the world. You are to be commended for taking your life's journey and using it as a way to light the path for others when it comes to Love. Black Love is essential to so many aspects of life. For instance, it plays an important role in building a strong foundation for creating Generational Wealth in the Black Community. When we Love, Build and Grow together, we Prosper together. Black Love also teaches young girls and boys how to respect and treat each other as they become Kings & Queens. In this day and age of Black Lives Matter, let's remember that Black Love Matters as well. And that Love begins within each one of us. Again, I am honored to be part of such an amazing tribute to Love. Although my Beloved Martin is no longer here in the physical realm, I can imagine that Million Dollar smile as I'm writing this. I can tell you from experience, it is better to have Loved and lost, than not to have Loved at all. Although as Spiritual Beings we really cannot "lose" anything. (Martin told me that. Wink.) When given the opportunity to Love, be sure to do it with all your heart. On behalf of myself and everyone who continues to believe in the Power of Love, we salute and give thanks for the couples presented on the pages to follow. Much Love!

Dedication

This Beautiful Book of Love stories is dedicated to my Sweetest Love, Perry. I'm so proud and blessed to have you as my life partner. Our path that led us to each other may not have been easy, but I can truly stand on these words: "I didn't go through all that for nothin'! " We have so many awesome examples set before us, to serve as roadmaps and compasses. We've also had the privilege of traveling our own journey. Sweetie, let's continue the path. For a life time. I also would like to dedicate this book to two of my favorite couples. My beloved Aunt and Uncle, ***Donald and Katie***. They celebrated 60 years of marriage in Year 2020 and are still going strong! I would also like to dedicate this book to my daughters' Grandparents, ***Gary and Terryl James***. They have been married 45 years as of 2021. As you navigate through these pages of love, you will get a glimpse of their story. As we repeat the theme of this story....

LOVE WINS!

"Chase what makes your heart sing."

Acknowledgements

As with every goal or mission I complete, I always first give honor to God. For without him, I Am Nothing. Next, I want to thank each of these beautiful couples for their transparency and for allowing us to peek into their love story. As we know…this is only a glimpse. I want to thank you for entrusting me with your "love". I appreciate the love that you have exhibited to the world and the real-life examples on how to persevere through it all. May each of you continue to thrive in bliss, in love, in your families and in each other. Mama—thank you for teaching your little girl about the love of reading and writing. You, beautiful lady was my first teacher. My first inspiration. I can never thank enough. Next, I want to thank my team who is always there to support me. Erin, your expertise and eagle eye in editng is one that I don't take for granted. Ericka & Erin Robinson; my Son-in-love, of ER Digital Marketing, I can never thank you enough for always giving me your time and expertise as well. Thanks for always capturing the vision of MyStory Publications for my book covers and all of my promos and websites. You're always so on it! And to all my family and friends who continuously support me, my mere words of Thanks is NEVERRRR enough. I'm so grateful to always have you in my corner. It means more to me than you'll ever know. I wish I could thank every person, one by one. I really do!

Black Love

What in the world is "BLACK LOVE"? My definition of Black Love is simple. It's the love that you see and adore in an African American couple. This same couple also shows genuine adoration for each other—like nobody's business! It's the kind of love that your Grandparents had back in the day. Was it a perfect love? Not at all. But it was the kind of love that weathered the storms and when the storms ceased, all the windows were still in place. The foundation was still solid. Today's generation, unfortunately, don't get the opportunity to witness this too often; at least that's my opinion. Black love: That couple who is so bound together that nothing can destroy their bond. At a very early age, perhaps, around the age of 16, I fell in love with love. I don't know why it was such a "thing" for me, but it was. I would prance in front of the mirror with my bubble gum machine ring on flaunting and waving my hand in the mirror. I was always in love with the idea of being married. Not sure why. But when I reflect, I do have beautiful memories of weddings that took place in my family. I remember vividly as a teen being a member of this particular church that really promoted marriage. They encouraged marriage as The Prize! I witnessed young couples fall in love and marry like it was the best thing in the entire world. This probably had lot to do with my view of marriage. It's absolutely not a bad thing. As a matter of fact, I pray that today, most places of worship do this as well. This seed needs to be planted in the minds of our young and youth at a very early age.

BLACK LOVE CONT.

No—marriage is not for everyone. However, they should at least be taught about the sanctity and sacredness of marriage and the true message of what God intended for this union. From television and the film industry, the portrait of marriage is not always painted on a beautiful canvas. We see celebrities flaunt marriage and toss it like it's nothing. Then, there's the whole discussion about pre-marital counseling and such. Do couples still honor this? Many will disregard this step in the name of, "We don't need that! I love you----and that's enough". When in fact, I wholeheartedly believe that pre-marital counseling puts the facts on the table. Good or bad. There are so many lessons to be learned not to mention, matters of the heart that MUST be discussed prior to the marriage. For example, blended families. If there are no ground rules put in place before hand, the bliss could turn into a burning fire very quickly! So, this is my urge to couples contemplating marriage---do the work, first. I sure wish I had in my early years. One last thing. My Dad recently gave some advice in regards to newly married couples. He said "it's sad when people get married and they lose the love. One should never go into a marriage with expectations. When you do, you'll always be disappointed. Just live day by day and trust God to be your provider, not a person. So, when something happens unexpectedly in the marriage---deal with it at that time. Have no expectations." Thanks Daddy! Excellent advice.

To the best 60 Years & Counting

The Reynolds

#Blacklove

60

YEARS

Katie & Donald Reynolds

How and where did you meet?

Katie: When I met Donald at Carver High in '57, I was in the band. I was still young and would walk home from school alone, so my Daddy always told me, "Don't stop and talk to nobody". And I didn't. I didn't realize that Donald was walking behind me, until one day he caught up with me to get acquainted. He asked, "Do you remember me?", and I responded, "No.", because I didn't. Still, I gave him my phone number, and the rest was history. My Daddy liked him right away. That made him special from the beginning. For our first date, he took me to the movies to see Imitation of Life.

Did sparks fly right away or did it take time?

Katie: For us, it kind of took time for sparks to fly. I was talking to someone else on the phone. We did not have much going on, because I heard that he had someone else pregnant.
didn't think that it would go far because I never dated someone who was dating someone else. I later found out that it wasn't true, so we started dating.

Donald: Well, I liked her from the beginning. She had the big legs. *jokingly laughs*. It was something about that that was attractive to me. She didn't like me at first, but later, I got a car and learned how to drive, and she's been driving my car ever since.

How long did you date before marriage?
We dated for over 2 years before we decided to get married in '60. We got married at Flipper Temple AME in Atlanta, GA.

How long have you been married?
We've been married for 60 years on November 29th 2020.

"No love can't last without the good Lord, Jesus Christ. That was my first love."

Katie & Donald Reynolds Cont.

How did you two deal with conflict within your marriage?

We focused on being honest with each other and expressing our feelings as we go. If we had arguments, we didn't have fights. Arguments don't solve anything. As we got older, we learned how to settle things with one another better. We always stayed together too. When we had problems, we never broke up but stayed together and worked through it. We had our own apartment as teenagers. In 1976, our place burned down and we lost everything. That experience taught us that we can always start back over from scratch if we have each other. Materials things weren't caught up in our relationship because we remembered that we started with nothing. That only strengthened the relationship.

Any tips on love and longevity?

Donald: No love can't last without the good Lord, Jesus Christ. That was my first love.

Katie: We also never went to bed mad and never got too proud to apologize. If you try to go to bed mad, you can't sleep. Most importantly, we always pray together.

Donald: You must be humble enough to change. I used to be out there in the world; but there were certain times where I had to be home. I got rid of friends that were not married and focused on my family.

Is there a word you live by or a foundational quote for your marriage survival?

Donald: I was taught that a man is not what he inherits, but what he gives up.
Katie: A quote for me is, "I can do all things through Christ, who strengthens me."

"As we got older, we learned how to settle things with one another better. We always stayed together too. When we had problems, we never broke up but stayed together and worked through it."

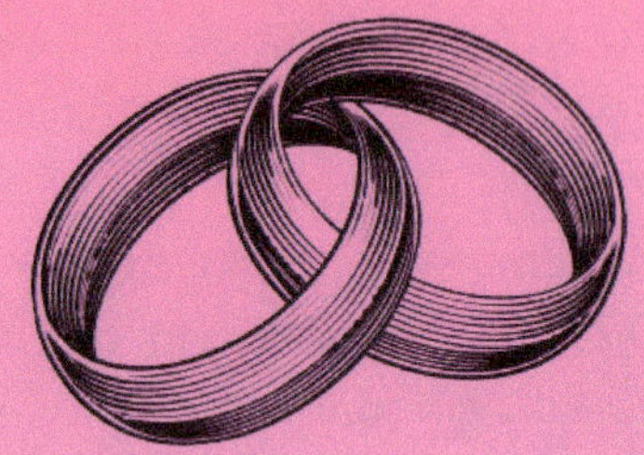

To the best 44 Years & Counting

The James

Grateful for It All!
#Blackexcellecnce

44
YEARS

Terryl & Gary James

How and where did you meet?

Gary: We met in Gatlinburg, TN. We were headed to a tourist site up in the Smoky Mountains. She found a situation to strike up a conversation. I think she saw me, and thought I was irresistible *Gary laughs*

Terryl: Well, I was playing coy. I asked my friend, "Who is the guy sitting back there by himself?", because I couldn't ask, "Who is that good looking guy?" Ladies just don't do that. He eventually moved from his seat up to my seat. He talked the entire time. He talked about sports and politics. He had real conversation.

Gary: I talked to her about political things and found that she was smart. She didn't just look good, but she was intelligent and could actually converse. That caught my interest.

Did sparks fly right away or did it take time?

Terryl: In my day, people were instantly falling in love. You could meet someone at 5 a.m. and be in love by 5 p.m. That was not the case here. When I first met Gary, I said no to seeing him again. I had a son and I had been married, so I refused to see him again. Each time he called, I said that I was busy and had something to do, but he just kept calling. He was persistent; so I finally said that I would see him again.

Gary: When I came to the house to meet her mother, she was very nice. I thought, "If her mama looks good, then she would look good when we grew old too." *laughs* Her mother thought that I was too young for her, but Terry had a job, she looked good, she was smart, had a car and a house, so I was persistent.

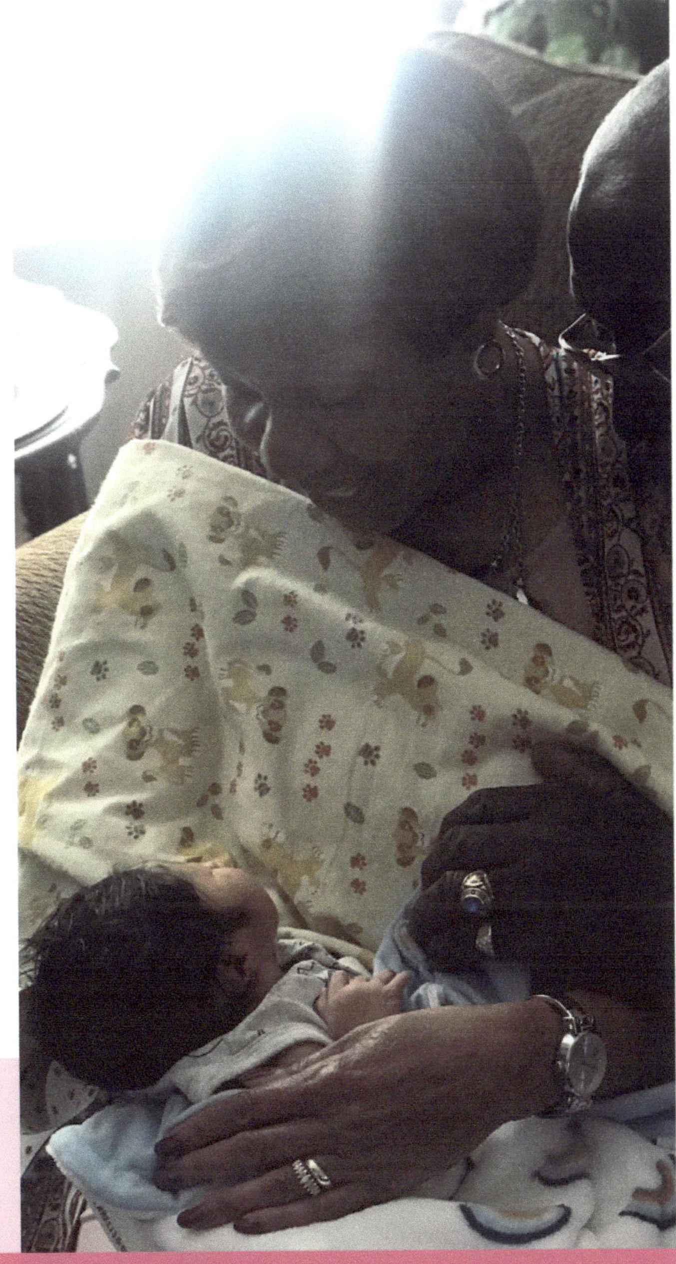

"Proverbs 3 verses 5 and 6 was the cornerstone for me for a number of years. Personally, it's easy to lean into my own understanding, you can assume and make things real to yourself. It reminds me to always depend on God to maintain your thinking.

Terryl & Gary James Cont.

How long did you date before marriage?

We met in '77 and got married in '78.

How long have you been married?

We've been happily married for 44 years.

How did you two deal with conflict within your marriage?

Gary: At one time, we didn't deal with conflict at all. Sometimes Terry would shut down because I wouldn't listen. It was either my way or the highway. We never disrespected each other, but we still didn't communicate well. I would make big purchases or take trips without consulting her. I learned over time that if you love a person, you'll begin to communicate and grow into compromise. You won't see it as a negative thing either. You'll see that you need to give and take. At first, I was kind of a chauvinist, and a little self-centered. I thought that the man makes the decisions. I learned to listen to her, and the longer we stayed together, it got better. In helping her raise Terrance (our eldest son), it was never an issue. My mom had 4 children when she married my stepdad, and when he came on as a Dad he pulled us all together. He was a good provider, very strict and very organized. So, I got a lot of traits from my Daddy and the things that I did not like I didn't do. I passed those things down to our son and he was very receptive to it.

Terryl: For dealing with conflict, one thing that was important to me was respect. Respect and communication goes a long way.

Any tips on love and longevity?

Gary: Well, life gets in the way, but you have to treat your wife like you're still dating her. You have got to show her affection all the time. My focus shifted from "What do I want?" to thinking about what she wants and what would be pleasing to her.

The scripture that stayed with me was Philippians 4:13. "I can do all things through Christ." Another important thing for me, was that I didn't get married to get a divorce.

Terryl & Gary James Cont.

Terryl: You have got to listen, not just talk. Pay attention to what your partner says and does. One day I came home with a belt for Gary. He says, "Honey I didn't know that I was going to get a belt", and I responded:" Well, you said you needed one."

Gary: And vice versa. When Terry needed a car, she didn't want me to buy her a Cadillac, but I wanted her in a nice and secure car. A luxury car because I like for her to have nice things or access to them. I will say that money helps, but also have transparency in dealing with your money. We had two separate accounts for a long time; I didn't see her checking for a long time, and she didn't see mine. You must be honest and upfront about finances.

Terryl: Lastly, prayer and our faith in God helps us. All these other things are good, but if you can't come together in your faith or have no prayer life, then you will lose. Someone has to have a connection with God.

Are there any words that you live by or a foundational quote for your marriage survival?

Gary: My spiritual life was the cornerstone for our marriage. When I did not want to tell her things, I would say " How would God want me to handle this?" It promotes the love in a relationship, so I don't feel like I'm trapped. I'm where I want to be and I'm not giving up anything.

Terryl: For me, some of them are, "Put God first in all we do" and "A family that prays together stays together." When we lost our youngest son, we were told that 90% of married couples get divorce after losing a child. People start pointing fingers to place blame on what you said or what you did. Proverbs 3 verses 5 and 6 was the cornerstone for me for a number of years. Personally, it's easy to lean into my own understanding, you can assume and make things real to yourself. It reminds me to always depend on God to maintain your thinking.

Gary: The scripture that stayed with me was Philippians 4:13. "I can do all things through Christ." Another important thing for me, was that I didn't get married to get a divorce. It was the folks that stayed married that we focused on, not those in failed relationships. I was raised to get married with the intent of staying there. Since 1973, I've had the same barber and go to the same bank. Like a marriage, it's better that you have a person that you love that's committed to you and you stay with them. I'm happy, blessed and thank the lord for that attitude.

The Holmes

"Keep it fun and find a way to laugh and get out to enjoy each other. Always remember what attracted you to that person in the beginning"

GERRI & KEITH

How and where did you meet?

On October 23, 1998 a friend, who's a singer invited me to her performance and asked me to bring some friends to a wedding anniversary party where he was to perform. One of my girlfriends in the group invited a guy she was dating. He invited 3 guys. Keith was one of them. All of the guys including Keith came over to our table where we were sitting along with the male singer and his friend. Keith had a dance with my sister and a friend of mine but for some reason we ended up at the table alone. I asked him "why hadn't you asked me to dance?" He responded, "I thought you were with the male singer". Once he realized I wasn't his date, we danced the night away. After the night ended, I gave him my business card (not mobile no.) For two weeks I did not hear from him. One day at work my friend received a message from her friend she was dating to inquire about me. The message from Keith was "What's up with her girl"? One Friday night we decided to meet out at a lounge in our area. Once again, we danced the night away. Even through some challenges on his end, his work schedule and my busy church life, we finally officially started dating.

Did sparks fly right away or did it take time?

Yes, there were undeniable sparks. We were definitely attracted to each other and realized we both loved to dance, so we danced the night away.

How long did you date before marriage?

We dated for four years before we tied the knot.

How long have you been married?

18 years.

How do you deal with conflict within marriage?

We discuss the disagreement and come to a solution to the problem and try to resolve it.

GERRI & KEITH HOLMES CONT.

Any tips on love and longevity?

Keep it fun and find a way to laugh and get out to enjoy each other. Always remember what attracted you to that person in the beginning and continue to reignite the sparks and allow all the positive energy and love you have for one another to outweigh any negative things in the relationship.

Words you live by or the foundation quote for your marriage survival?

Do not allow "Distractors" to come into your relationship. Distractors are people or things that keep you from focusing, maintaining and continuing your relationship.

FORMAL NIGHT OUT

1999 -WHEN WE WERE DATING

OUR BEAUTIFUL GRANDCHILDREN

The Taylors

DIA & DARRELL TAYLOR

How and where did you meet?

We met at the Democratic National Convention in Atlanta, Georgia in 1988. I was selected as a Page for GA Democratic Party Delegation for my hard work and dedication on the campaign for Congressman John Lewis. During this time, I was a Sophomore. Darrell was out of college and was working for Bellsouth as a technician. He was guarding the communications equipment on the last night of the convention near the GA delegation and spotted a young woman wearing a black and white polka dotted dress, white stockings, and hi-top white sneakers. We talked for hours and laughed at some of the entertainers that evening. We were both amazed with the history that we were becoming a part of that night. Darrell never asked for my phone number but he did give me his pager number, cell phone number, and phone number to his Aunts home where he was living at the time.

Did sparks fly right away OR did it take time?

Darrell: No, it took time. It took about three weeks before I even received a call from Dia. When she did call, I had forgotten who she was. She basically had to reintroduce herself again. It was at that time we continued to talk and get to know one another.

Dia: It took me about three weeks to call him because I was a fulltime college student and I remembered that he gave me his phone number one night when I was at work. He told me he almost didn't answer the phone because he didn't know why he was getting a phone call from the Day's Inn Reservation Center. We dated for the remainder of my time in college and really got to know each other, my family adored him, and eventually I met his LARGE family after a trip to his family home in South Georgia. By the time we hit my senior year, I knew he was the ONE. Afterall, how could I not be in love with someone who would drive 30 minutes to bring me hot french fries from McDonalds while I was studying for final exams!!

DIA & DARRELL TAYLOR CONT.

How long did you date before marriage?

We dated for about 2 years before he asked me to be his wife! He drove limousines part time while we were dating and one night, he picked me up after he dropped off his passengers. I just knew this was the night he was going to ask me to marry him, but NOPE!

We drove around I-285 highway. He dropped me off at my mother's house, kissed me on the cheek and said goodnight. After that I was about ready to walk because some of our friends were getting engaged all around u and I didn't understand what was taking so long LOL. I think he asked me to marry him about 1 month after the limo ride.

How long have you been married?

We celebrated our 30th wedding anniversary in August 2020. Unfortunately, due to the pandemic, we couldn't celebrate in Italy as planned.

How do you deal with conflict within the marriage?

Conflict is inevitable. but combat is optional! (Max Lucado). We try to keep the lines of communi cation open and work hard to speak out of love and not anger in the midst of conflict. We both have pretty strong personalities and opinions and these tra its make for interesting and healthy conversations when we don't agree.

Any tips on love and longevity?

Keep dating, try new things together and get away as much as your budget will allow so that you can strengthen your connection to each other. Hang out with other couples who share a common interest and will help to edify and strengthen your marriage! Give what you want to receive! Fry chicken butt baked together at least once. It builds trust. Your spouse is not your problem! We learned this after completing a 6 week marriage boot camp through Radical Love.

Words you live by or the foundation quote for your marriage survival?

Marriage is the process of developing unconditional love-the very nature of God. The greatest marriages are built on teamwork, mutual respect, a healthy dose of admiration and a never-ending portion of grace. 2 Corinthians 12: 8-10.

The Forresters

LARRAINE & MICHAEL FORRESTER

"Today, kisses are sensuous, satisfying, and mean much more than they did during the early years of our marriage. However, there was a period in which the rare kisses we shared were purely physical, no true meaning; our kisses were only intended to bring physical fulfillment. Today we have over 35 years of kisses under our belt. Over the years in addition to our kisses we've spent time loving, laughing, fussing, fighting, resetting and restoring. In our earlier years, we enjoyed with great passion the mere presence of one another. Initially our relationship was long distance which meant that we spent many late-night hours on the phone talking about our days, our interests, and our dreams. We were both excited when we had the opportunity to see each other in person, look into each other's eyes, touch and kiss."

Michael was raised in a home with a loving mother and father who made the decision to move from Kingston, Jamaica to the United States for their family. The family settled in Miami, Florida. His Mom and Dad taught their children to command respect and pursue success. Michael's mother was indeed the nurturing mother who used her wisdom to teach her children both domestically and intellectually. Michaels father, a true provider in every sense of the word, worked both hard and smart as he cared for his wife, his children, his family. Michael's family was well established and stable and didn't struggle in any way.

Larraine spent her formative years with Mom, Dad, and siblings in Georgia. Their family was filled with love and fun. Larraine's father laid a foundation for Larraine to understand and embrace her value as "Daddy's little girl". He taught her two older brothers that they were to love, protect and honor her. She took that same teaching and used it in her relationship with her younger brother with whom she developed a very strong bond. Larraine's mother, a strong woman had to become even stronger when Larraine's father passed away and left her to raise 4 children alone. It was from her mother that Larraine learned to be strong.

LARRAINE & MICHAEL FORRESTER CONT.

Michael came into the marriage with the intellect given by both his mother and father. Unfortunately, He also brought a generational curse of infidelity. Larraine came into the marriage as Daddy's little girl who was entitled to having things her way and an attitude of a strong woman who desired, but didn't need a man. The first nine years of marriage were great. The fact that Larraine's son was 5 when they married didn't present any insurmountable problems; blending the family was relatively easy. Planning the birth of a second child was also easy even though Michael, a US Soldier at the time, received orders to deploy to Korea during the pregnancy. The distance endured, only enhanced desires to be together and enjoy more passionate kisses and expressions of love for each other. Thanks to their OBGYN, Michael was able to get leave to fly home for the birth of their second child.

"During the first nine years of our marriage many of our peers perceived us to have a dream relationship. However, perceptions can be a bit deceiving which was evident to our close friends and relatives. It was during this time that Michael made bad decisions and entered entanglements that positioned his kisses to land on the lips of another. We both did things that could have possibly caused the destruction of our marriage. We both considered, desired, and did the paperwork to dissolve our marriage. Even after the kisses that brought about the conception of our third child, we had much to learn about what it would take to have true love and longevity in a marriage.

For us, in some seasons, divorce seemed to be the only option. Our marriage has not been one where we said: "I do" and we lived happily ever after enjoying kisses sweeter and sweeter each day. We had to learn to be intentional about our love and about our kisses. We had to learn to love each other and teach each other how we wanted to be loved. We've always enjoyed a sweet, sensuous kiss from a physical perspective. Our kisses have always allowed us to taste the milk and honey under our tongues, but the sweet sticky honey wasn't enough to hold us together as husband and wife. Considering the invested years at the worse period of our marriage, neither of us wanted to throw in the towel, give up and position our children to be labeled as children from a broken home. We ultimately made the DINAO™ decision, that is for us Divorce Is Not An Option.

Because we made that decision, we were able to triumph over bad attitudes, disrespect, infidelity, and drug addiction to name a few of our trials. We promised God that if he saved our marriage and pulled us out of the pit of hell which was a dysfunctional marriage, we would always be available to help other couples. God did answer our prayer and we have upheld our commitment. Through our Pre-Marital program titled DINAO™, we have counseled many couples in hopes of helping them learn to communicate effectively, budget wisely, parent with principles, consistently implement spiritual disciplines, stay together and always kiss passionately.

We've also had the honor of uniting over 700 couples in Holy Matrimony and declaring them C.U.T.E. Committed, Unmovable, Trusting and Exalting God. We believe that God created the institution of marriage and we will always give him the glory for the joy that we have in our marriage. We stand on our foundational scripture "All things work together for the good of those who love the Lord and are called according to His purpose." Romans 8:28

Together we now enjoy our family which includes our three adult children, their mates and our three grandchildren. The two of us spend quality time together and with our offspring's. We count it a blessing that we haven't given up on each other nor will we ever give up on love. We enjoy watching movies, playing cards and board games such as Scrabble, Pictionary, and Backgammon. Occasionally we workout and travel together. We also enjoy kissing!"

The Johnsons

JAMILA & DWAUNE JOHNSON

When and How you met?

August 18, 2002: We met at Salem Missionary Baptist church one Sunday morning while running late to get in the choir stand. Dwaune stopped me and asked me my name and that was it. Admittedly I had seen him at church before and thought he was cute. It was several Sundays later that he walked me out to my car and mentioned it was dirty. I replied that he should come clean it and that's how he got my number.

How long did you date?

We unofficially dated/but were friends for two years. He had been in a bad relationship and had trust issues. I was ready before he was but looking back on it, I realized that time with it being just me is what I needed. As my friend mentioned, she had never known me not to be with anyone. I think that was time for both of us to heal from past hurts and really get to know ourselves. We 'officially' begin dating in 2004.

Did sparks fly right away?

We were definitely attracted to each other.

How did you both know he/she was the one?

There was no lightning bolt for me. I just knew that I enjoyed being with him and when he wasn't around, I was sad. As an only child I value my ME time but after some time I realized that I wanted him in my space all the time.

How long have you been married?

We were married on August 19, 2006 so a little over 14 years.

How do you deal with conflict within the marriage?

We are both spiritual and always try to pray for and with each other. Communication is important but sometimes it doesn't always go well. Marriage is definitely a daily job with no days off.

Any tips on love & Longevity?

Learn each other's Love language. It's important to understand what the other person desires and understand why they do/act how they do. Surround yourself with like-minded couples. Keep family and friends out of your marriage and household decisions. Seek Spiritual counsel when needed.

Words you both live by, or the Foundation quote for the Survival of your marriage

1 Corinthians 13: 4-13. The Chapter on love.

1914

The Johnsons

Charlotte & Darin Johnson

When and how did you meet?

In December 2006, Darin moved to Atlanta, GA from Kansas City, MO. At that time MySpace was the most popular social media platform available in which to connect with friends and family. One day, I received a private message stating that he had just moved to the area and would like to make new friends locally. He and I continued to message back and forth and before you knew it, we were in the New Year. We formally met in February. Darin and I were both invited to a Super Bowl party with the game matching up between the Chicago Bears vs. Indianapolis Colts; February 2007. He came with his brother and I came alone. We ate, played games, and enjoyed watching the game. Charlotte shares, "After the party, we stayed in contact casually in the coming months as just friends. The next face to face contact occurred in August at my birthday party held at my home. The contact was brief as Darin had busy obligations that day. We continued to communicate over the next few months without any in person contact. I told Darin that I was scheduled to have surgery shortly after Thanksgiving. Darin wasn't previously aware, so we made arrangements to hang out prior to the surgery. We ended up going to see a movie and out to dinner. We spent time and enjoyed each other's company before giving well wishes and parting ways for the night. Even though we were not officially together, we classified this as our actual "first date".

The next evening after the surgery, Darin called to check on me.. He did not expect me to answer and was planning to leave a message.. However, I answered. He was checking in on me and kept it brief since he knew I was resting. After that time, we began seeing each other often. Numerous times. We officially began seeing each other exclusively on December 7, 2007. After this, we began routinely seeing each other after work- multiple times per week." Over this time, the relationship continued to grow. However, we experienced some doubts."

There were doubts at times about the longevity of the relationship. Charlotte was coming out of a relationship that had lasted for a decent amount of time. She loved the other gentleman and had even expressed that she didn't believe that she would fall in love with Darin because of the seriousness of the previous relationship. Despite this, Darin remained persistent to win Charlotte over until she eventually fell in love. "A full year into the relationship, we became officially engaged. This occurred on a dinner movie date. It was quiet and privately done for the most part with few people noticing-- but it was still a great moment in our relationship. The courting continued as we also planned for a wedding to take place the next year. On December 5, 2009, we were officially married. Our honeymoon took place in Myrtle Beach, SC shortly thereafter. Even though the weather was cold and we couldn't really enjoy the beach, our celebration was beautiful. Over the years, we have experienced our ups and downs but remained close, persistent and always there for one another.

"Our tips would be to continue to date each other multiple times a month. Continue to express interest in each other.

Charlotte& Darin Johnson Cont.

How do we handle conflict?

We handle conflict by talking it out and working through it--if it is something that can't be resolved right away.

Any tips on love and longevity?

Our tips would be to continue to date each other multiple times a month. Continue to express interest in each other.

Words you both live by, or the Foundation quote for the Survival of your marriage To keep God in the center. Always communicate regardless of feelings because communication is key. Stay positive and have a positive outlook rather than a negative outlook. Forget the happy wife, happy life theory. It's happy spouse happy house, because marriage is not 50/50, marriage is a give and a take because when one is without, the other is pulling all of the weight. Always be supportive, listen to hear and not to respond. Never go to bed mad and always say, I love you. After 13 years of being together and 11 years married, we now have 2 children. By the grace of God, we are still going strong with more growth, prosperity, intimacy, unconditional love, and most of all, good times to come!

The Hoods

Angela & Lawrence Hood

How and where did you meet?

We met in 2016 on an online dating site. We talked every day for a month before we actually met. We really learned a lot about each other by talking every day. By the time we actually met face to face it seemed like we had been knowing each for years.

The Date

While getting to know each other over the phone we realize that we both were jazz enthusiast. There was this jazz club in Conyers, Ga owned by renowned jazz saxophonist Kim Waters called "Kim Waters JazzTones Cafe". We decided to meet there and the rest was history. We laughed, talked ate dinner, danced, met Kim Waters and were the last ones to leave the establishment. However, as we were leaving Lawrence said "I have something to tell you." He had been setup on a blind date prior to meeting me and it was the next day. I found this to be interesting. However, I appreciated his honesty.

The next day which was Saturday, Lawrence called at 5:00pm and said he was home from his blind date. He stated that he explained to the lady that he had met someone that he was really interested in and wanted to give the relationship his full attention. Lawrence asked me what was I going to be doing Sunday and I said I was going to church. He asked could he go and I said yes. We have been attending church together ever since.

How long did you date?

We dated for 1 year. We did everything locally from the movies, plays, concerts, dinners which sometimes included hotdogs from the Quick Trip. However, one day he asked me "if you could go anywhere in the world where would you go?" Without hesitation I said "Paris". He said "Paris?" and I said you asked. Two weeks later, Lawrence said "if I ask you to go to Paris with me would you go?" I said "yes!" and the rest is history.

"Lawrence asked me what was I going to be doing Sunday and I said going to church. He asked could he go and I said yes. We have been attending church together ever since".

Angela & Lawrence Hood Cont.

Did sparks fly right away?

Yes, from the moment we physically met I felt as though I was introduced to my soul mate. He says he felt the same way.

How did you both know "he/she was the one?

Lawrence always says "He couldn't get rid of me" lol. I said when I stopped asking God for what I wanted and decided to ask God what did He want for me, that's when I met Lawrence.

How long have you been married?

3 years.

How do you deal with conflict within the marriage?

We both were previously married and wanted to do things differently. We decided to go to pre-marriage counseling. We learned about the 5 love languages. We identified and studied our individual styles together.

Now when there's conflict we try to communicate through each other's love language style which is really effective for us.

Any tips on keeping the love alive?

Lots of prayer. Stay Respectful. Pick your battles. Keep the relationship spicy. Date night isn't option it's mandatory. Honesty and Communication. Always be honest and make every attempt to communicate effectively.

Words you both live by, or the Foundation quote for the Survival of your marriage.

Psalm 19:14 Let the words of my mouth, and the meditation of my heart, be acceptable in thy sight, O Lord, my strength, and my redeemer.

"He couldn't get rid of me" lol. I said when I stopped asking God for what I wanted and decided to ask God what did He want for me, that's when I met Lawrence.

The Millers

Cynthia & Anthony Miller

When and how did you meet?

Anthony Miller and I met February 16, 1996 on a blind date. My ex-sister-in-law, which is his cousin introduced us. I was young, freshly divorced and swore I would not ever fall in love again. Anthony was looking for someone who had a strong Christian background and had a love for children. The evening of February 16, 1996, we met at Dugan's in Stone Mountain, Georgia and later went to a Valentine party my family was hosting in Thomaston, Georgia. Once we got back in town, we exchanged numbers and talked on the phone for hours at a time. We were taking it slow because at the end of the day, if the relationship did not manifest, we wanted to remain friends.

Did sparks fly right away?

No, sparks did not spark right away because I was freshly divorced with a five-year old daughter. To add fuel to the fire, after three weeks of knowing each other, I found out I was pregnant with my second child by my ex-husband. This threw a monkey wrench into our relationship, which prompted him to step away and let life take its course. I knew things were over with my ex-husband. However, at the same time, I also knew what it looked like and if I was in Anthony's position, I would have cut ties with me as well. Two months had passed with no contact before our paths crossed again. I was on my lunch break in Buckhead where fate had our paths to cross again. He motioned for me to roll my window down, which I happily obliged. After our conversation, I instantly knew he was the one because, "What man was willing to deal with all my baggage?" At that point, the rest is history.

" Marriages have roots that are deep, solid covenants, sweet love, and obstacles, but GOD IS GOOD!

Cynthia & Anthony Miller

How long did you date?

We dated for two years, before we married May 2, 1998, and turned around and did it again March 20, 2010.

How did you both know he/she was one?

Cynthia: I knew Anthony was the one when he accepted that I was pregnant with my ex-husband's child. I think he was able to deal with it because the pregnancy occurred prior to us meeting.
Anthony: I knew Cynthia was the one because she was not in the streets or at the clubs. She was all about her family and church life.

How long have you been married?

We have been married for 22 years with daughters; ages 30 and 24 and a 19-year-old son.

How do you deal with conflict within the marriage?

Communication is key. Anthony has been in law enforcement for nearly 20 years, which makes communication a priority. It took time for us to listen and understand what each was saying, instead of just responding to get our points across. As time went on, we attended marriage counseling to teach us how to communicate with one another. We also worked on how I personally needed to deal with the stress of having a husband in law enforcement, who deals with the stress of his occupation. In return, we also realized we were not each other's enemy. We are #teammiller#5.

Any tips on love and longevity?
Love, Pray and Play together. We both have our flaws, but who doesn't? Pick and choose your battles. Some are not worth discussing. Also, travel and make plenty of priceless memories.

Words you both live by or the foundation quote for the survival of your marriage?
Love is what is does.
Cynthia: Respect is fuel for a husband in order for him to be the man God created him to be for his family. Don't leave your husband on empty.
Anthony: Never let anyone get closer to you other than your spouse. If someone can get close to you, they have the opportunity of destroying your relationship. Marriage is not just love. It is communicating, compromising, providing, trusting and understanding.
The Millers: Marriages have roots that are deep, solid covenants, sweet love, and obstacles, but GOD IS GOOD! Our marriage allows us to annoy each other for the rest of our lives and we love it!

My Favorite Quote is by Mya Angelou:

"A woman's heart must be so hidden in God that a man has to seek HIM to find her!"

My Favorite Scripture:

Romans 8:28 "And we know that all things work together for good to those who love God and to those who are the called according to His purpose." "In everything give thanks." Both "bad" and good (Romans 8:28)

This scripture is soo idea because when we dated long distance from 2015 through 2016. It was hard, but we pressed and made attempts to see each other on a monthly basis. In the Spring of 2016 he moved to Atlanta to prove his love for me...he had no job but trusted God. And though I had reservations .... God had a bigger plan, and that plan was for us to "go through to get to". August 8, 2020 Lennell arranged a surprise engagement party and asked to take my hand in marriage. I can't say it was an easy ride from 2015 to 2020, because we had to learn each other...but the hard, rough times paid off because we are planning to be married this year of 2021!! With GOD, All things are possible!!! Matthew 19:26 #LoveJones2021 #TeamUs

Congratulations To The Future Mr. & Mrs. Jones!

LaTonya Pouncey & Lennell Jones

In continuation and in celebration with all of the beautiful BLACK LOVE stories, The MyStory Publications family would like to extend a big ole congratulations to LaTonya Pouncey and Lennell Jones on their engagement and future nuptials. We certainly wish you a lifetime of God's love, His peace and His covering over your marriage.

LaTonya shares their story: Lennell and I met in Chicago on December 26, 2014. We met at a party that he was promoting. Of course, I didn't know him, neither did I know that he was promoting the party until he walked up to me to see if I was having a good time. Then he explained he was the promoter. I told him that I came to this event with some of my Chicago Friends. Explaining that I am a native of Chicago, but I have been living in Atlanta since August 1991. He basically told me that he would like to keep in touch with me and offered his business card which was in his truck. He went to get the business card, gave it to me, and asked me for my phone number; which I shared with him. Needless to say, the rest is history. He told me that he knew I was the one when he saw me from a far. After conversating, I found that his deceased mom and I both share the same birthday of February 22nd and we favor a great deal. Lennell relocated to Atlanta in Spring of 2016 and we got engaged August 8, 2020. God knew what HE was doing for sure!!!

The Whaleys

"Let Love Happen."

Our Love Story

Love is truly amazing. Two friends, who rescued each other by finding true love. This pretty much sums up our amazing love story.

We met in 2015. I was shopping for a new car. Perry was a salesman at the dealership. I so love telling this story because ONLY GOD could orchestrate a story like this. I literally heard him before I saw his handsome face. He carries a "boom" in his voice. Almost like a radio voice. He was with a customer returning to the car lot from a test drive. But he was calling out to another colleague–VERY LOUDLY. Even though he was very loud, there was something about his voice that caught my attention. I truly believe it was his energy more than anything. At this point, I quickly turned around to see who this loud man could have been! Then, I saw his face. He has Vitiligo. At the time, I didn't even know the proper name for his skin condition. But I do recall saying to myself... "Good for him". By that I meant, he apparently had such a zest for life that he did not allow his condition to affect his attitude. I instantly was more intrigued.

After making my purchase, I asked the Finance Representative "who's that guy with the skin condition". She immediately said "You don't know Perry?" You need to meet Perry." So naturally, I'm REALLY set on this introduction. Prior to that conversation, she and I had chatted about my career, and my passion for my Women's empowerment organization. Afterwards, she went looking for Perry, but he was gone for the day. It was a few weeks later that I would finally meet, my now King. I returned to the dealership for a follow-up action for my vehicle. He walked through the waiting room, and this was the beginning of our destined friendship. I asked if he had a moment to speak with me. With all his energy, he quickly said "Sure! Come to my office". We went through all the preliminaries of getting acquainted. I was single at the time and was hoping to meet someone to just simply hang out with---so I asked eagerly "Are you seeing someone?"

He hesitated at first. Which still tickles me today. But he soon thereafter, quickly nodded his head and said YES. I'm in a relationship. I was disappointed, but it meant nothing for me to back away because I have high regard for marriage and relationships. I also wanted to respect his lady. But as fate would have it, we ultimately became the best of friends. I quickly learned that Perry was well loved and respected all over the city of Atlanta. He had been serving in the capacity of motivational speaker and mentor for the Vitiligo Community spreading Awareness. My admiration for him grew 1000 times over! I felt it an honor to assist in any way I could. This is how our friendship grew. Amazingly, it was always platonic, and we were always strictly friends over the years. I don't think we ever really gave a second thought to the first day we met. We continued to work and put forth efforts in giving back to our community.

Again, as fate would have it, we both married other people and ironically divorced around the same time. I was completely outdone with this news because he never shared anything about there being this possibility in his marriage. So, I was surprised. Even after hearing the news, I used some of my relationship coaching skills to encourage him in possibly working through his marriage. Nevertheless, to no avail. On both our ends. As time would lend, we continued working together, but somehow in the process, we started holding hands. Lol. We have absolutely no complaints about it at all.

Perry has come to mean the world to me. I've never been in love with my best friend. It's a beautiful thing and I'm forever grateful to God for bringing us into each other's lives. In this discovery period of our lives, we both learned that we had experienced marriage at a very young age, and when it wasn't successful, we gave it a try at least 2 additional times. I was in complete awe that God would connect me with someone who completely understood my story without judgement. Because of this revelation, we were able to collaborate and write a book titled; "My Three Wives; Lessons Learned on Choosing A Mate". This book would mirror my recently published book titled; "My Three Husbands; Key Points to Know Before Saying I Do".

This experience has been absolutely amazing. I now sign all of my books with a simple note of advice. "LET LOVE HAPPEN". I'm so grateful that we did. I truly believe in marriage and the sanctity of what God designed it to be. No one ever marries with plans to divorce. But LIFE HAPPENS and we encourage people to never give up o love.

Perry asked me for my hand in marriage 2 weeks before Christmas. He asked if he could marry me on my birthday in 2021. I said YES!

This by far has been the best love story of my life. My prayer is that we use ALL the lessons learned and key points to gain a love like no other--- for a lifetime.

www.ingramcontent.com/pod-product-compliance
Lightning Source LLC
Chambersburg PA
CBHW040452100426
42813CB00021BA/2981